Business Development And Growth Strategy For Beginner

Scaling Up Your Entrepreneurial Journey
And Building A Path To Lasting Success
In A Competitive Market

By

Gray S. Bergan

Copyright

All rights reserved. No part of this publication may be distributed, or transmitted in any form or by any means, including photocopying, recording, or other electronic or mechanical methods, without the prior written permission of the publisher, except in the case of brief quotations embodied in critical reviews and certain other noncommercial uses permitted by copyright law.
Copyright © (Gray S. Bergan), (2024).

Disclaimer

The information contained in this book is for general informational purposes only. While every effort has been made to ensure that the information provided is accurate and up-to-date, [Gray S. Bergan] makes no representations or warranties of any kind, express or implied, about the completeness, accuracy, reliability, suitability, or availability of the information contained in this book for any purpose. Any reliance you place on such information is therefore strictly at your own risk.

In no event will [Gray S. Bergan] be liable for any loss or damage, including without limitation, indirect or consequential loss or damage, or any loss or damage whatsoever arising from the use of this book.

About The Author

Gray started small but became a big deal in business and finance. His interest in economics as a young person made him dive into learning about money and how it shapes society. Instead of settling for a regular job after doing well in school, he explored various fields to soak up knowledge. He learned about different businesses, from new startups to big financial companies. But Gray didn't just want to understand things; he wanted to change them. He believed financial knowledge should be for everyone, not just for the elite, so he became a writer sharing what he knew with experienced business owners and people starting out. What made him special was his knack for explaining tricky money ideas in an easy way. He also saw how technology could transform banking, so he fully embraced it, pushing for new ways to mix digital tech with old-style banking to make businesses better and more efficient.

TABLE OF CONTENT

Introduction: A Comprehensive Guide to Corporate Growth   **9**

   The Significance of business development for beginner   10

   Constructing the Conditions for Achievement   12

Chapter 1: What Is Business Development?   **14**

   Strategies for Business Development   15

Chapter 2: Recognizing the role that scalability plays in the expansion of businesses.   **22**

   Factors Affecting the Scalability of Businesses   23

   Challenges in Expanding a Business   27

Chapter 3: How to overcome the obstacles that come with expanding a business   **31**

Chapter 4: ESTABLISHING SUCCESSFUL BUSINESS OBJECTIVES   **43**

   The significance of establishing objectives for your business   43

Chapter 5: Writing a Business Growth Plan   **56**

   How to draft a strategy for business expansion   58

   Why are strategies for business expansion important?   64

   What elements affect the expansion of a business?   66

   How a strategic strategy is developed   69

Chapter 6: Market research and analysis   **83**

    How can you tell whether market research is necessary?   83

    How to carry out market research   88

    How to carry out a market study   91

    What is the role of QuestionPro in market research? 96

    How to Present Analysis and Research on the Market 98

Chapter 7: Marketing and Sales Techniques   **103**

    Marketing strategies that attract and retain customers 106

Chapter 8: What is social media marketing and how should your strategy be developed?   **125**

    Advantages of Social Media Marketing   126

    Top Social Media Marketing Techniques   132

Chapter 9: KPIs, or Key Performance Indicators, to Help Grow Your Business   **137**

Conclusion   **159**

Introduction: A Comprehensive Guide to Corporate Growth

Businesses in today's fast-paced market need to constantly grow and adapt if they want to stay competitive. But what is their approach? Growth in business might assist with this.

Sustainable growth is also required for successful corporate development; growth on its own is insufficient. To provide a solid basis for future success, it involves making strategic investments that add value and uniqueness. Whether via product releases, market expansion, or the creation of strategic relationships, business development is crucial to a business trajectory and long-term success.

The Significance of business development for beginner

Not only is it useful for individuals launching their own enterprises to understand the principles of business development, but it is also essential. This explains why:

1. Building a Sturdy Foundation: Sound business development lays the groundwork for constructing a solid foundation upon which an organization may expand. By creating a strategy plan, establishing specific objectives, and doing in-depth market research, novices may position themselves for long-term success.

2. Accelerating Growth and Innovation: Business development encourages both growth and innovation. By consistently finding and using new opportunities, businesses may remain competitive, adapt to changing market circumstances, and foster a creative culture that drives long-term growth.

3. Resource Maximization: One of the key goals of business development is to increase the efficient use of resources. Efficient allocation of resources is necessary for both sustainable growth and operational optimization. This includes human resources, financial resources, and technical infrastructure.

4. Creating Value for Customers: At the end of the day, a successful business growth plan is about generating value for customers. By learning about the needs, preferences, and pain points of their consumers, businesses may develop products and services that address real-world issues and provide meaningful solutions. This encourages long-term success and fosters strong client loyalty.

Constructing the Conditions for Achievement

It is crucial that you establish a solid foundation for your path to commercial success before diving into the abundance of information that awaits you in the next chapters. Developing the correct mentality and psychologically preparing oneself for the difficulties and accomplishments that lie ahead are also important aspects of this crucial period. Education is not the only thing covered.

It's an exhilarating experience to launch your own business, but you also need to temper your excitement with humility. The knowledge that building a successful business takes time, patience, and tenacity is one example of realistic expectations. A business's route is usually characterized by sluggish growth and occasional setbacks, even if stories of unexpected success sometimes make headlines. You may overcome hurdles with resilience and concentration if you understand that success is a process rather than a destination. Success as an entrepreneur mostly stems from having a growth mindset, which is an outlook that embraces challenges, sees failures as opportunities for progress, and believes in the possibility of continuous improvement. It takes curiosity, resilience, and a reframed view of failure as valuable teaching opportunities to approach problems with a growth mentality. Instead of seeing failures as insurmountable barriers, view them as stepping stones toward success. When you see problems as opportunities for improvement, you and your business will both benefit from having a growth attitude, which will instill confidence and motivation.

Chapter 1: What Is Business Development?

Business development is a strategic process that aims to increase an organization's profitability, growth, and expansion. It entails seeing and seizing chances that fit the goals of the business. This multi pronged strategy includes relationship-building, market research, and strategic alliances in addition to traditional sales and marketing.

It seeks to proactively explore new markets, products, and partnerships in order to build a sustainable future. It entails studying consumer demands, assessing market trends, and setting up the business to successfully address those requirements. Business development specialists are essential to the company's success because they make the connection between its internal resources and outside prospects.

Strategies for Business Development

Business development should be a part of any business overall development plan if it hopes to expand. You may enhance your brand in a variety of ways. For achieving your objectives, some may be more effective and useful than others. Finding those that enable you to reach your goals is the primary responsibility.

1. Take use of networking possibilities

You must look for fresh chances and make the most of your resources if you wish to grow. You may establish alliances, reach out to new customers, and enter new markets. You must devise a special strategy to achieve these objectives.

2. Build trusting connections with clients

In this day and age, when technology plays a major role in businesses, consumers often do not have genuine interactions with brands to help them choose the best solution and guide them through the onboarding process. Nonetheless, businesses still need communication with their clientele. Maintaining openness, integrity, and trust is essential. To better understand your customers, do market research and provide tailored offers, promotions, discounts, and other offerings.

3. Contribute to local communities and charities. Think about collaborating with other successful businesses to engage in philanthropic activities. A rising number of well-known companies are worried about social and environmental issues. They support a wide range of communities. Remember that you must choose a group that is aligned with your goals and aspirations. For example, if your business opposes animal testing, choose a community that shares your concerns about animal welfare.

4. Utilize social media

Both businesses and customers find it impossible to envision their lives without social media. These social networking platforms enable business owners to create connections and commercial contacts. Facebook, LinkedIn, and Instagram are great tools for product promotion, consumer outreach, and sales. To give you an example, you may configure SendPulse's chatbot for Facebook Messenger if you utilize Facebook. In this manner, you may respond to inquiries, assist clients with the checkout process, and resolve certain technical problems.

5. Put referral schemes into action

Referral programs are something to think about if your business has great client loyalty and a stellar reputation. Your clientele will assist you in expanding your network of current and prospective clients. Thank them for introducing you to friends.

You'll have more sales, money, and clients as a consequence.

The process of business development

Businesses may find, evaluate, and seize growth opportunities with the aid of the Business Development process, a flexible and rigorous approach. This framework for strategic planning includes a variety of interconnected activities that all contribute to the ultimate goal of achieving improved profitability and sustainable development. The following is a definite explanation of the process:

1. Determine possible points of contact

Finding possible growth possibilities is a critical first stage in the business development process. This calls for a thorough examination of the business environment, including trend analysis, market research, and a sharp eye for new opportunities.

Through careful examination of customer behavior, technology developments, and market gaps, businesses may identify unexplored markets and sectors that are well-positioned for growth. This first stage is crucial because it establishes the framework for the strategic choices that follow and guarantees that resources are directed toward the areas that have the best chance of succeeding.

2. Clearly define your objectives

Specific goals and objectives should be established after the study so that the business may strive toward them. These include establishing income targets, establishing growth goals, concentrating on gaining customer targets, and establishing goals for the creation of new products and services. These objectives enable the experts to concentrate on

3. Encourage the development of thought leadership

Establishing credibility with the individuals they will or are doing business with is one of the most crucial steps in the Business Development process. you must position yourself as a leader in this industry in addition to being a valuable individual contributor. By providing your clients with in-depth blog material, you may accomplish this process and gain their confidence as a subject matter expert. Additionally, your vast knowledge will be able to spread more widely, which will eventually trickle down to sales.

4. Look into potential leads.

You have to investigate your leads in great detail throughout this phase. This implies that you should find out whether they are trustworthy if you wish to collaborate with them or if you intend to do business with them in the future. Effective handling of cold leads is also possible, but you must use caution while converting them into leads.

Chapter 2: Recognizing the role that scalability plays in the expansion of businesses.

The ability of every firm to grow is critical to its sustained success. It refers to the ability of a business to grow and succeed without being limited by the structure of its organization or the availability of resources. Businesses that prepare for scalability may increase revenue, enhance overall performance, and better handle growth.

Not only can scalability be used to grow a business, but it can also be used to gauge its success. Scalability is a sign that a firm has established a strong base and implemented effective procedures. It shows how a business may adjust to changing market conditions and maintain an advantage over rivals.

On the other hand, there may be hazards if scalability is not planned properly. These consist of ineffectiveness, obstructions, and even the incapacity to take advantage of fresh chances. This might thus lead to lower profitability, a decline in market share, and eventually stagnation.

Therefore, for businesses hoping to achieve long-term success and continuous expansion, scalability must be understood and addressed.

Factors Affecting the Scalability of Businesses

The scalability of a firm is influenced by many things. Let's examine how market dynamics and technology affect an organization's capacity to grow.

A. Technology

The way organizations run has fundamentally altered as a result of modern technology, which also increases efficiency and allows for potential expansion. With the right IT infrastructure and tools, businesses can simply expand their operations, automate processes, and streamline workflows.

1. Cloud computing: By allowing businesses to store and access data and apps over the internet, this method eliminates the need for physical servers and infrastructure. This reduces costs while giving businesses the flexibility to expand or contract as needed.

2. Digital platforms: Allow businesses to reach a global audience and penetrate new markets. Companies may reach a larger audience and transcend regional borders by simply listing their products or services on online marketplaces.

3. Data analytics: By using data analytics tools and processes, organizations may get crucial insights into customer behavior, industry trends, and operational performance. More specifically, they may identify opportunities for growth, concentrate on a particular customer base, and modify their strategies to meet the demands of the market.

B. Market Situation

Market circumstances have a significant effect on a business's capacity to grow. A firm that operates in a market that is highly competitive or changing swiftly has to be flexible and able to react to changes fast. Economic variables, client tastes, and market demand all affect how well a corporation may grow. A company may find it simpler to grow in a market where there is a ready market for its goods or services and there is less competition. However, scaling may need unique approaches and individuality to stand out in a crowded market with fierce competition.

C. Customer Preferences

Scalability is also significantly influenced by customer choices. Businesses must adjust to changing customer tastes and preferences by providing goods and services that meet these evolving needs. Through continuous observation of customer preferences and trends, firms may set themselves up for future expansion and scalability.

D. Aspects of the Economy

Scalability of a firm may also be affected by economic variables, such as interest rates, rates of inflation, and general market stability. Businesses may find it difficult to grow during recessions because of declining consumer spending and unstable markets. On the other hand, when the economy is doing well, firms could find it simpler to grow since customers are more inclined to spend and have more discretionary cash.

Challenges in Expanding a Business

While scalability offers several advantages, it also poses some challenges. Let's look at the many challenges that expanding businesses may face.

1. Identify Possible Scalability Issues.

Early detection of issues with scalability is crucial. Businesses need to anticipate potential bottlenecks and take proactive measures to address issues like inadequate resources or inadequate infrastructure. Failing to identify and handle scalability issues might impede a business's ability to grow and flourish overall.

2. Getting Rid of Scalability Barriers

Overcoming scaling issues often requires adaptability and inventiveness. Businesses must be prepared to implement efficient processes, make strategic adjustments, and invest in infrastructure.

Scaling solutions need to be regularly reviewed and improved in order to ensure long-term success.

How to expand your business

You may begin expanding your business by implementing these three steps.

1. Evaluate the market's demand for your products or services. Before thinking about scalability, you need to determine a few important features of your business:

Is a problem resolved by your business?

Which market may there be for your offering?

The answers to these questions often go hand in hand because, if enough people are experiencing a certain problem, a solution may benefit some of them. This suggests a substantial target market and shows demand for your business, allowing you to effectively create your own market.

Similarly, if there is a large enough market for the products or service existing, then inefficiencies in the product's quality or customer service are undoubtedly existent. This is an opportunity.

Investors look at a number of criteria, including the market's size and the company's ability to respond swiftly to changes in the market by scaling up or down. For these reasons, you need to ascertain your total addressable market.

2. Establish mechanisms that help your firm expand.

Establishing the procedures and systems necessary to support your firm expansion is a prerequisite for scaling. Your business may not be able to meet the extra demand that comes with expansion without these systems and procedures.

Thankfully, automation in data and finance management, content marketing, and human resources is now possible thanks to technology. Investing in technology may come with an initial expense, but the benefits will accrue over time.

3. Determine what you can contract out.

It's crucial for business owners to focus on their strengths and outsource everything else. Since you can't do everything on your own, it's critical to support your firm with a robust sales staff, administrative team, and customer service department. Start giving your staff the freedom to decide for themselves and assume leadership positions inside the business. In this manner, you may keep your attention on the advanced work required to expand the business.

Chapter 3: How to overcome the obstacles that come with expanding a business

Numerous obstacles impede expanding companies. various possibilities and difficulties call for various answers as a firm expands; what worked a year ago may not be the best course of action now. Preventable errors often result in an average firm from what might have been an excellent enterprise.

If you want your business to develop and prosper in the future, you must identify and avoid the frequent dangers that come with expansion. In particular, you must be certain that the activities you really do now don't prompt further issues. Under the guidance of a capable leader, you can fully capitalize on the opportunities and create sustainable, long-term growth.

certain risks and mistakes that often affect growing businesses, along with remedies.

1. Staying current with the market.

2. Making preparations in advance.

3. Financial management and cash flow.

4. Solving problems.

5. appropriate systems.

6. Competencies and dispositions.

7. Accepting Modification.

1. Staying current with the market

When you first start your firm, market research is not something you conduct on a one-time basis. Since business circumstances are always changing, so too should your market research be ongoing. If not, you face the danger of basing business choices on outdated data, which might result in the collapse of your company.

As you achieve more success, rivals become more aware of your actions and respond accordingly. A deal that leads the market one day might turn out to be just mediocre after a few months.

Apparently dedicated clients rush to recognize different sellers offering a superior deal.

Sales growth and profit margins are constrained when items (and services) age. Determining the current stage of your goods' life cycles might assist you in determining the best way to increase overall profitability. Investing in innovation is also necessary if you want to create a steady flow of new, lucrative items for the market.

2. Making preparations in advance: The strategy that worked for you a year ago may not be the best one for you right now. The state of the market is always changing, therefore you should periodically review and revise your business strategy.

Your plan must adapt as your business expands to accommodate your new situation. For instance, you may start concentrating more on creating lucrative connections and fostering development with current clients rather than just acquiring new ones. Pre-existing company partnerships might provide consistent cash flow as well as higher profit potential. While the turnover in newer connections could be higher, the profit margins might be lower, which might not be sustainable.

Every business must simultaneously be on the lookout for fresh chances. There are clear dangers associated with depending just on current clients. By spreading out your clientele, you may reduce those dangers.

Expanding a firm using the same concept is not the only way to achieve growth. Better development chances may be found with alternative strategic choices like franchising or outsourcing.

It's crucial to remember that just because you're successful now, it doesn't imply you'll always be able to seize these chances.

Avoid being too opportunistic by considering if fresh concepts align with your capabilities and your overall business plan. Recollect that there are in every case new risks related to new turns of events. It's important to periodically assess the dangers you face and create backup strategies.

3. Financial management and cash flow

Effective management of cash flow is crucial for every kind of organization. It's critical for a corporation that is expanding since financial limitations may be the largest barrier to expansion and excessive trading may be lethal.

Optimizing your financial resources need to be a fundamental component of business strategy and opportunity analysis. If chasing these chances will deprive your primary firm of vital funds, you could have to turn down excellent prospects due to resource constraints.

It is important to closely monitor every aspect of working capital in order to optimize your free cash flow. Tight command over past-due bills and proficient credit the board are vital. Raising capital against trade obligations is something else you may wish to think about.

As a firm expands, efficient supplier management and good inventory control usually become more crucial. Obsolete stock holdings might develop into an issue that has to be cleaned up on a regular basis.

You could choose to switch suppliers and systems that can manage just-in-time delivery, or collaborate with providers to shorten delivery cycles.

Anticipating your financial requirements in advance enables you to get appropriate funds. Whether to bring in outside investors to supply the equity required to support future development is a crucial issue for many expanding firms.

4. Solving problems

New businesses are often in a state of constant crises. The majority of management's time is spent troubleshooting since there are new difficulties every day that must be resolved immediately.

This strategy just doesn't work when your firm expands. Even while a short-term crisis is always essential, there are other things you may be doing that could be more important. While spending time calming down a displeased client may help preserve that one relationship, your efforts would be better served by hiring the appropriate salesman, who might give the basis to critical new deals long into the future. As your firm expands, you must also be aware of emerging issues and concerns.

For instance, if you don't take action to make sure your intellectual property is adequately safeguarded, your business may be more and more in danger. You may need to invest more in building your brand if you are concentrating on particular marketing efforts. Determining the primary forces behind development is a useful method for determining priorities.

Building your business plan, managing staff, and leading personnel are the main objectives of a disciplined management style. You create structures and processes that make problems simpler to address in the future rather than treating each one as an isolated incident.

5. appropriate systems

A lot of data is delivered and utilized by all organizations: Monetary records, correspondences with clients and other business partners, faculty data, lawful requirements, etc. without the appropriate frameworks, it's an excessive amount to make due, not to mention use productively.

As your business expands, jobs and responsibilities may be assigned, but efficient management is impossible without reliable management information systems. It becomes more difficult to guarantee that information is exchanged and various departments collaborate efficiently as your firm expands. Establishing the proper infrastructure is crucial to promoting the expansion of your business.

Policies, processes, and documentation all gain importance. In a developing firm, the casualness that could be appropriate with one or two staff and a small number of clients is just impractical. You need appropriate employment processes, precise terms and conditions, appropriate contracts, and so on.

Using established management standards is one of the greatest methods to introduce best practices, according to many expanding firms. Implementing quality control methods may play a significant role in promoting enhancements and persuading bigger clients of your dependability.

Placing cash into the proper framework is a venture that will take care of over the long haul. Every day, more efficient operations benefit you. In the event that you want to sell the company, showing that you have effective, well-run procedures will be crucial to establishing the business's worth.

6. Competencies and dispositions

The powers behind beginning and extending new ventures are business people. Much of the time, they are additionally the ones keeping them from pushing ahead.

The skills you need to help your business expand are different from those that may assist you in starting it. You must be careful not to deceive yourself into thinking too highly of your own ability. Almost certainly, you will take preparation to obtain the capacities and outlooks important for somebody driving advancement.

You must learn how to effectively delegate, have faith in your management team, and relinquish day-to-day control over every aspect of your business if you want it to flourish. Excessive intervention may easily hinder drive and creativity. You'll also need to hone your time management abilities and learn to prioritize your tasks as the company becomes more complicated.

Perhaps the most troublesome thing effective business owners need to learn is the way to pay attention to and acknowledge guidance. If you want to make use of your possibilities, however, it can also be necessary. A couple of business owners even assign another person to act as executive or overseeing chief when they understand their own cut off points.

7. Accepting Modification

A rising business may be seriously threatened by complacency. It is highly foolish to assume that just because you have been successful in the past, you will continue to be successful.

You may be reminded of the shifting market circumstances and the need to adapt by periodically reviewing and revising your business strategy.

Chapter 4: ESTABLISHING SUCCESSFUL BUSINESS OBJECTIVES

The key to selecting business goals is to make sure they are realistic and challenging. As an organization, set quantifiable goals like a 10% rise in online sales instead of overarching objectives like "increase revenue" or "improve customer service." Make sure your business objectives are S.M.A.R.T. (specific, measurable, achievable, relevant, and time-bound) when choosing them.

The significance of establishing objectives for your business

Why are objectives important? For the following reasons;

1. Objectives provide direction.

As a business owner, there are many goals you want to achieve. What are the most crucial jobs, though? How can one determine if they are progressing?

You may prioritize your work, give yourself direction, and provide a framework for measuring progress by creating well-structured objectives. There will be no more haphazard tasks or side pursuits—just a clear understanding of your goals and the path to achieving them.

2. Objectives inspire and unite your group.

Taking up tasks aimlessly does not result in success. There is no bright light in front of you that you are attempting to attain if you don't have a goal. There are no landmarks along the route to commemorate and motivate you.

Setting and achieving team and corporate objectives increases motivation. Additionally, it makes it much simpler to establish personal objectives that relate each worker's efforts to the main purpose.

3. Objectives provide a framework for evaluating success.

When you set objectives, you have to think about the metrics you'll use to assess your progress. By doing this in advance, you can monitor your progress far more easily and determine if you're still on course.

If you skip the goal-setting process, your definition of success will continue to be nebulous and unfocused. You may never really achieve your goals and are more inclined to go down fruitless rabbit holes.

4. Objectives aid in the development of your business.

Setting objectives boosts your odds of obtaining consistent business development, just as developing a business plan increases your chances of successfully beginning a firm. You'll know exactly where you want to go, how to get there, and if you're making progress.

Setting, reviewing, and revising your objectives consistently can also help you to expedite the process and steer clear of expensive errors.

Your business strategic objectives

It's critical to concentrate on the objectives that will bring your vision or purpose closer to reality. Strategic objectives are helpful to many firms when they are attempting to make judgments about productivity that will benefit their corporation. There are several sizes, dimensions, and formats for strategic plans. There is an actionable plan out there to match each objective you are working toward.

A strategic goal: what is it?

Strategic objectives are plans for your business that provide qualitative or quantitative outcomes. This implies that reaching the objective has to be something you can quantify and monitor using statistics, such as higher numbers, higher earnings, or higher rates of productivity. Examples of goals and objectives in strategic planning come in a variety of forms that might be helpful. Which objectives you decide to pursue will depend on what will be most advantageous for both you and your business.

For short- or long-term objectives, some organizations choose to construct comprehensive strategic plans, while others just use a basic framework. While some strategic plans are more intricate and incorporate many levels, others have straightforward aims, strategies, objectives, and tactics. The amount of accountability you want to achieve, the timescale you want to finish them in, and the culture of the business will all influence how the strategic objectives are developed. Whichever approach you use, the most crucial element of defining strategic objectives is coming up with a strategy and sticking to it.

How to formulate immediate business objectives

Generally speaking, short-term business objectives are ones that you hope your business will accomplish in the next weeks or months. When establishing short-term company objectives, you may take the following actions:

1. Determine the short-term business objectives for your organization for a certain timeframe.

The first stage in creating short-term company goals is deciding which objectives you want to accomplish within a certain time frame. A lot of short-term objectives are ones that help long-term objectives get closer to completion. Convert your long-term objectives into short-term goals that will advance your company by taking into account your short-term objectives and what you want to achieve in the next weeks or months.

2. Divide every mission into doable business targets.

Each short-term goal should then be divided into manageable targets. These goals need to outline the measures your business will take to accomplish each one. For instance, if your purpose is to acquire six new clients during the next month, your goals will be the actions you will do to win over those six clients, such placing a fresh advertisement in a newspaper and publishing content on social media three times a week.

3. Make sure your goals can be measured.

Measurable business goals must be established in the preceding phase. Don't just say "post more on social media" as a plan, for instance, if one of your goals is to increase the number of posts you make there. Rather, be as explicit as you can to make the goal quantifiable. You may take the example above, "post on Facebook twice a week and Instagram three times a week for eight weeks."

4. Assign staff duties relating to the aim.

Once the goals for each short-term goal have been determined, assign each goal to a team member or employee who will see it through to completion.

5. Regularly assess progress

Track your short-term objectives' progress on a regular basis to make sure you are on schedule to complete them within the allotted time. Measure any extra customer or prospective customer engagement you get as a consequence, for instance, if you raise your social media postings to three times a week as part of a business objective. To better accomplish your goals, monitor your progress and change your targets as necessary.

Short-term business objective examples

A few instances of short-term business objectives are as follows:

1. For the next three months, raise the price of the products by 3%.

2. Over the following five months, hire three additional staff members for marketing.

3. Boost interest in your company's blog.

4. Conduct freebies for clients on social media every month.

5. Launch a program for "Employee of the Month" awards.

6. To start funding a charity, choose one.

7. Make an account on a fresh social networking platform.

8. Post on social media three times a week on average.

How to establish enduring corporate objectives

When establishing long-term business objectives, you should also take into consideration the following actions in addition to the ones listed in the section on how to develop short-term goals:

1. Decide what you want to achieve in the following ten years.

Identifying the objectives you want to achieve over the following several years is the first step towards developing long-term company goals. It is common knowledge that ten years is enough time to make objectives, but you may also set goals as far ahead as twenty years or as close to the present as one year. Determine and record as many objectives as you can for your company to accomplish within the time frame you have chosen.

2. Set long-term business objectives as a top priority.

Many businesses have many long-term objectives that they want to achieve. But it's challenging to concentrate on many objectives at once. Because of this, it's critical to rank the goals you want to concentrate on highest and allocate corporate resources toward achieving them before tackling other objectives.

3. Divide all long-term goals into manageable short-term goals.

You must divide your long-term goals into manageable short-term targets, just like you would with short-term goals. For instance, you must divide your long-term aim—raising your company's total brand awareness—into manageable short-term goals that will eventually enable you to reach your long-term goal. Three weekly social media posts and a monthly collaboration with social media influencers are two examples of achievable goals for the aforementioned aim.

4. Regularly monitor your business long-term objectives.

Setting and maintaining frequent goals is crucial to achieving long-term objectives. Long-term objectives might be difficult to remember or lose sight of since they may take a while to accomplish. It's possible to make necessary modifications and make sure you're headed in the correct direction by monitoring your progress toward each objective.

Long-term business objective examples

Some examples of long-term business objectives are as follows:

1. Over the following two years, raise your company's overall revenue by 10%.

2. Cut manufacturing costs by five percent during the next three years.

3. amplify the awareness of your brand overall.

4. Boost the market share of your business.

Chapter 5: Writing a Business Growth Plan

Running a business makes it simple to lose yourself in the present and concentrate exclusively on the tasks at hand. But if you want to be really successful, you have to prepare for expansion and look forward to it. A business development plan is something that many business owners draft in order to plot out the following year or two and determine how and when sales will rise.

A business growth plan describes the goals for the next one to two years. entrepreneurs use a growth mentality while developing strategies for revenue development and expansion.

Plans for business expansion should be prepared periodically. The corporation has the opportunity to evaluate the business objectives it met and failed to meet at the conclusion of each quarter. The company development strategy may now be updated by management to take the current state of the market into account.

What ought to be included in a business development strategy?

A business development plan is primarily concerned with growth and the strategies you'll utilize to get it. It takes time to develop a good strategy, but maintaining your development trajectory may provide significant rewards.

The following components must be part of your development plan:

1. An explanation of the prospects for growth.

2. financial objectives laid out by year and quarter.

3. A marketing strategy that outlines your development objectives.

4. A financial strategy to ascertain the funds available for expansion.

5. A summary of the duties and requirements for personnel at your organization.

How to draft a strategy for business expansion

Writing a corporate development strategy effectively requires study and forward-thinking. When creating your company development strategy, keep in mind these important guidelines.

1. Plan ahead.

The future is never certain. You may, however, prepare for future development if you research your competitors, your target market, and the historical growth of your business. A thorough advice on creating a business plan for expansion is available from the Small Business Administration (SBA).

2. Examine other development strategies.

Review successful firms' models before you begin writing.

3. Find areas where you can improve.

You may find out whether your growth prospects are best served by developing new goods and services, expanding into untapped markets, setting up additional offices, or going worldwide, to mention a few, with a little investigation. Include your top growth choices in your strategy after you've determined what they are.

4. Assess your group.

A review of your workforce and an analysis of the number of personnel needed to achieve your growth goals should be part of your strategy. You may work out how much more you can get done with your current team by evaluating your own and your workers' talents. Along with knowing what skill sets to look for in those new workers, you'll also know when to step up the recruiting process.

5. Spread the word.

Expanding your business requires focused marketing. Make sure to include a description of your business's successful marketing strategy, including how it will grow and change as you do.

6. Request assistance.

When crafting your development strategy, advice from other entrepreneurs who have experienced profitable expansion may be the most helpful resource.

7. Put pen to paper.

Writing development plans has been made easier by business plan software, which offers templates you can customize with data unique to your business and sector. The majority of software packages are designed for generic business plans, but they may be readily adjusted to produce a plan that emphasizes expansion.

Don't worry if you don't have business plan software. A company development plan may be made using Google Docs, Microsoft Word, or another comparable program. Make the following parts for each growth opportunity:

1. What is the chance? Is a new product, a new consumer niche, or a new geographic expansion your growth opportunity? How are opportunities identified? Incorporate your market research to prove the feasibility of the concept.

2. What aspects of this opportunity are important right now? Your development opportunity may, for instance, make use of cutting-edge technology, profit from a clever alliance, or seize a market trend.

3. What are the opportunity's risk factors? Determine the elements that might make implementing this growth potential difficult. The general status of the economy, fierce rivalry, or problems with supply chain distribution are a few examples of obstacles.

4. What is your strategy for sales and marketing? Determine the sales and marketing strategies that will enable you to take advantage of this expansion opportunity. Give specifics about your message, potential sales ideas, and the marketing channels you plan to employ (print, social media, etc.). For instance, you may arrange distribution agreements with pertinent brick-and-mortar or internet stores or recruit sales representatives into a new region.

5. What are the expenses associated with this expanding field? For instance, you may need to purchase additional raw materials and production equipment if you introduce a new product. While marketing expenses are unavoidable, don't forget to account for additional sales expenses like commissions. Describe any economies of scale or locations where the new expansion sector is less costly than a stand-alone endeavor due to your current activities.

6. What will your cash flow, spending, and revenue look like? For the following three to five years, project your revenue and costs and create a cash flow statement specifically for the new growth region. Provide a sales estimate, a break-even analysis, and a breakdown of all anticipated costs to determine the net profit increase from the new project. Describe how the new growing area will affect current sales, either favorably or adversely. For instance, you will probably sell more bathing suits if you decide to expand your line of business and start selling cover-ups and sunglasses.

Following the completion of this task for every development opportunity:

1. Make a summary that takes into consideration all areas of progress over the time.

2. For a complete view of the situation and its effects on the business, include condensed financial statements.

3. Analyze the finance required to carry out the strategy, taking into account a range of possibilities and interest rates.

Why are strategies for business expansion important?

Here are just a few of the many factors that make business development strategies crucial:

1. Market share and penetration: You will inevitably begin to report losses rather than profits if your market share stays the same in a world where expenses are always rising. Plans for business expansion assist you in averting this situation.

2. Making up for early losses: In their early years, most businesses lose significantly more money than they make. You'll need to expand your business to the point where it can generate enough income to settle your obligations if you want to recover these losses.

3. Minimizing future risk: Growth strategies are important for well-established companies as well. These businesses can always improve the efficiency and liquidity of their sales. If you need cash on hand to meet unforeseen expenses, liquidity might be very helpful.

4. Attracting investors: Attracting investors is the main goal of a business development strategy for the majority of businesses. Describe to investors how your business intends to increase revenues in the next few months.

5. Concrete revenue strategies: Growth plans don't have to adhere to a predetermined template; they may be tailored to each organization. All company development strategies, however, need to place a strong emphasis on income. A basic inquiry such as, "How does your company plan to make money each quarter?" should have an answer in the plan.

What elements affect the expansion of a business?

Think about these important elements that might affect the expansion of your business:

1. Leadership: Understanding the ins and outs of your company processes and how outside influences affect them is essential to achieving your objectives. Without this information, you won't be able to lead and develop your staff to increase income, and you'll see stagnation rather than progress.

2. Business owners: Small business owners are inherently engaged in management, which includes securing capital, assets, and both digital and physical infrastructure. Your capacity to carry out these responsibilities will be impacted by inefficient management, which might impede your progress.

3. Customer loyalty: Gaining new clients may cost five times as much as keeping existing ones, and a five percent improvement in retention can result in 25–95% higher profitability. These figures show that a company's ability to retain customers is essential to its expansion.

Which four main growth tactics are there?

There are many different kinds of corporate development plans, but there are basically four main kinds. You may decide how to strengthen your brand with the help of these growth tactics.

Market strategy: This is the plan you have for reaching out to and influencing your target market. This approach is about making the most of what you already have, not about branching out into new markets or developing new goods and services to increase your market share. Could you, for example, change your price? Is it time to start a fresh marketing initiative?

Development strategy: This approach entails investigating methods for introducing your goods and services into untapped markets. One objective may be to enter a new market if the existing one isn't providing the growth you're looking for.

Strategy for diversification: Diversification entails broadening your product offerings and target markets. Smaller businesses with the resources to be flexible in the goods and services they provide and the new markets they want to enter are often the most suited for this approach.

How a strategic strategy is developed

Your strategy will be better if your basic planning is more detailed. A development phase precedes the actual drafting and creation of a strategic plan. Keep in mind that crafting this phase might take weeks or even months. To avoid ambiguity and misunderstanding, this has to be very well-written, well researched, and thorough.

The procedures for creating a strategic strategy are as follows:

1. Examine market, customer, and rivalry trends.

2. Conduct a SWOT Analysis.

3. Compose a mission statement.

4. Make a statement about your vision.

5. Establish your short- and long-term objectives.

6. Establish departmental goals and core values.

7. Define the needs for workforce, finances, and budget.

1. Examine market, consumer, and rivalry developments.

Aligning with the organization's stated purpose and objectives is the first stage in the organizational strategic planning process. Analyzing market, industry, and competitor trends comes first in this process. Starting this procedure with an external rather than an internal assessment of your business characteristics is the best course of action. Among the concepts you need to research for your analysis are:

1. The magnitude of your corresponding sector

2. trends in prices.

3. licensing, governmental regulations, and other possible problems.

4. Trends in products.

5. concerns raised by customers about goods and services.

6. Threats and competitors, along with what they have done in the last six to twelve months

7. Rate of industry growth.

The majority of this data is easily accessible. Once more, your plan will become more effective the more comprehensive and well-researched these sections are. Two of the most important things are to distinguish your brand from competitors and to have a top-down understanding of the business.

2. Conduct a SWOT Analysis

After addressing the research component of your strategy, you need to create a SWOT evaluation. This study assesses the opportunities, threats, vulnerabilities, strengths and weaknesses of you, your team, or your business. Similar to several other strategic planning procedures, it is crucial to provide sufficient time to offer a comprehensive evaluation of every facet.

1. Strengths: Consider what makes you superior to others in the field. What sets you apart from the competition might include a highly trained workforce, substantial money or cash resources, investors, industry development, minimal entry hurdles, a clientele, and a profit margin.

2. Poor staff training, low profit margins, high entry barriers, and a small customer are some of the weaknesses. The SWOT approach might be helpful in brainstorming ways to enhance areas of weakness.

3. Opportunities are places where you, your group, or your business can succeed. Opportunities include things like willing and eager investors, patents, new product offerings, brand awareness from other products, and anything else that presents an opportunity for success.

4. Threats: Anything that has the potential to harm your business is a threat. Market dynamics, consumer spending power, cash flow issues, or declining product pricing are a few examples of these.

Both internal (strengths and weaknesses) and exterior (opportunities and threats) aspects are the focus of the SWOT analysis. During this phase, it's critical to utilize this and other analytical techniques to get a clear knowledge of your situation and the objectives you should pursue.

3. Compose a mission statement.

Creating a mission statement may assist your company in identifying objectives and strategies for achieving them. By outlining the organization's basic beliefs and purpose for being, a clear and concise mission statement may clarify matters for all members of your team. The foundation of strategic planning is these two elements.

The majority of businesses publish their mission statements online for clients to see as samples of statements you may use to guide your own. Look up the mission and basic principles of your favorite companies on the internet. Mission statements come in various lengths. The purpose is to discuss your business mission and the services you provide to clients.

4. Make a statement about your vision.

How you plan to carry out the mission statement should be outlined in your vision statement. Make your vision statement understandable to everybody by eliminating industry jargon and terminology. A vision statement serves as motivation for staff members as opposed to external parties like investors or clients, unlike a mission statement. Your brand's values, objectives, purpose, and mission will be upheld and maintained by creating a vision statement.

Your own vision statement may be made by responding to the following inquiries:

1. After five to 10 years, where will the brand be?

2. How will my business engage with clients or enhance their quality of life?

3. What effect will my firm have on the sector? the globe? customers?

You may create a vision statement that details your future goals after you've responded to the questions above.

5. Establish your short- and long-term objectives.

You should create both short- and long-term business objectives after finishing the SWOT analysis and identifying the company's basic values. Short-term objectives are benchmarks that will enable you to reach long-term objectives, which should be in line with the company's mission statement. Setting clear, relevant objectives may be facilitated by using the SMART goal structure.

Although your objectives should be unique to your business, the following are some instances of areas where goals might provide value:

1. increasing the effectiveness of operations.

2. Building a corporate culture.

3. increasing the income.

4. Modifying or improving the available products.

5. assisting with fresh approaches to marketing and sales.

Establishing a goal that is both tough and reachable is crucial. It's also a good idea to have a way to gauge your progress toward your objectives.

6. Establish the department's goals and fundamental values.

Development of fundamental values is another facet of strategic planning. These may work in the other way as well as aid in crafting your purpose and vision statements. This implies that you may ascertain your basic values with the aid of your vision and purpose statements. Typically, an organization's core values are encapsulated in one or two sentences that express its guiding principles.

Examples:

1. Sincerity.

2. Superior quality.

3. Dependability.

4. Integrity.

5. passion.

6. Diversity.

Departmental goals may be derived from these fundamental principles. Departmental goals are an essential aspect of company strategic planning and aid in the development of strategy. All of these goals need to be established annually so that your group may accomplish them and make any required adjustments in the next few years.

7. Specify your demands for workforce, finances, and budget.

Your strategic plan's last section should include the personnel, funding, and budgetary requirements necessary to meet the objectives. Determining what each department will need to fulfill their portion of the organization's objective should be a team effort.

Typical parts of a strategy document

The following are the typical components of a strategic plan, however your plan may include other aspects based on your organization's needs:

1. Executive summary: In the executive summary, briefly state the goal of your strategic plan. This has to be succinct and direct. Sometimes it helps to write this part last so you can finish the concepts in a few phrases and it will be fresh in your head.

2. This is the page where your strategic plan will be signed off on by all high-level stakeholders.

3. Business description: This might be useful for setting the scene by giving some background information on the firm, its goods, and services. Emphasize the brand's relevant accomplishments that relate to the goal.

4. Mission and vision statements including core values: To strengthen your mission and vision statements, you may also include core values in this part.

5. SWOT and strategic analysis: Your SWOT analysis and any other significant research that shapes the remainder of the strategy should be included to present your objectives and strategies.

6. Action plans: Clearly state in your action plan how you intend to carry out your vision and objectives within the allotted period. Be specific in your activities and in how you implement the strategy for the whole organization.

7. Operating and financing budget: Accountants or finance specialists may assist you in estimating the amount of money required to fund your action plan. Add things like anticipated cash flow, revenues, costs, return on equity, and any potential debt you may have.

8. Providing a thorough evaluation criteria for your strategic strategy is important. This can include reviewing year-end financial data, getting input from clients, conducting staff interviews, and more. Give a brief explanation of how you intend to gauge the plan's performance in one or two phrases.

9. Implementation: This should include how you intend to present the strategy to the relevant departments, staff members, and people. All the stakeholders in your team and in management should get this part. Every person should be able to articulate exactly how, in relation to their role, they contribute to the strategy. They ought to know what it takes to succeed in carrying out their mandated duties.

10. Feedback and scorecard: Although optional, a feedback or scorecard area could let staff members and management ask insightful questions on how the strategy is doing. For most individuals, a scorecard is a more effective visual tool than a written record.

Chapter 6: Market research and analysis

Regular market analysis is a crucial part of managing any successful organization, since it offers valuable insights about the business current and future state. This study includes primary and secondary research, industry and market statistics, customer satisfaction, opinions and purchasing patterns of consumers, and more. It also includes qualitative and quantitative marketing research.

How can you tell whether market research is necessary?

It might be difficult to know where to begin when there are so many opportunities for insights. Examine your top business goals to see whether any of them may use fresh information and insights, and then decide what kind of market research you need.

These are the two questions you should ask yourself.

1. Do you possess the knowledge required to achieve your objectives?

2. Are those statistics current and complete?

If one of the answers is negative, then current research insights will help your plans.

The Importance of market research to your business

You may learn a lot about buying trends, the most popular services across different demographic groups, and other topics from your client data.

You can forecast future changes in the industry and identify important trends with the aid of market research. **The following are some of the factors that make market research crucial for your business:**

1. finds new goods and services

You may use market research to help you figure out what new goods or services the market needs and how to provide them. It is possible to identify the main problems with creating a certain good or service, which can help you steer clear of expensive development errors.

It also helps you figure out what aspects matter most to consumers and how to incorporate those aspects into products you want to sell.

2. finds potential clients

Your understanding of your clientele may be improved by knowing their gender, age, income, profession, and way of life, among other demographic details. You can target your present clients in the future if you know who they are. Ineffective product performance might result from marketing to the incorrect kind of consumer.

3. Determines the feasibility of a product or service

If your business intends to introduce a new product or service, you must first assess the market's readiness. Will consumers like the product? Do you wish to contact clients that need the product? How likely is it to succeed, and will it be feasible?

4. keeps your business one step ahead of rivals.

Comparative studies are a great way to monitor the advancement of your rivals in relation to your business.

This is a great chance for you to find out what they are doing differently than you if they are much ahead of you. You may create business plans to keep one step ahead of your rivals.

5. lowers risk and increases revenue

With the right information, you can lower the risks your business faces and decide which risks, given current and projected market trends, are worthwhile.

Determining the feasibility of a market via market research reduces the likelihood of failure. Reducing risk also requires knowing what your consumers need. Ultimately, reducing risk contributes to higher profitability.

6. Aids in comprehending current clients

Because of their complexity, your clients may not need what you used to need. You have to keep an eye on the health of your clientele if you want to succeed. You may get more insight into your present clientele by doing market research.

Customer satisfaction levels are also determined in part by the market research. If you find out why they aren't satisfied, you may address the issue. If it's high, you can determine why and discover strategies for maintaining it that way.

7. Assists in establishing reasonable objectives

You may use up-to-date information about your clientele and market to develop reasonable objectives. You can really build that development and know what to anticipate in the future when you establish a pattern of progress throughout time.

Achievable goals can help you save money, get started sooner, and miss out on more beneficial long-term objectives for your business.

How to carry out market research

1. Decide on a focus.

Establishing your research goals should come first. Perhaps you should:

Recognize your target market.

- Create fresh features for your products.
- Establish a unique brand identity.
- Enhance the experience for customers.

Understanding consumer sentiments around sustainability, for instance, may be your main goal when introducing a new line of environmentally friendly packaging.

2. Choose your research techniques.

Based on your goals and financial constraints, decide how you'll collect the data. To comprehend attitudes and opinions, combine quantitative data from surveys with qualitative research from focus groups and interviews.

Perhaps you will choose to interview customers who care about the environment in a focus group to find out how they feel about the materials used in packaging.

3. Gather the information

You may need to develop questionnaires, conduct interviews, or evaluate data sets, depending on your study methodology. To expedite the process, you may either carry it out internally or contract it out to a third party.

4. Examine the information

It's time to transform that unprocessed data into knowledge now. Find any trends or patterns that address your goals. You may, for instance, research and determine what proportion of consumers choose eco-friendly packaging over conventional choices.

5. Share your results.

Write a report with the most important information, figures, and suggestions derived from your research. Don't only report the results; but discuss the implications for your business. In terms of your product, audience, or market, what conclusions can you draw?

For instance, you might draw the conclusion that a focused marketing effort aimed at the 25–34 age range could boost sales if your research reveals a significant demand for eco-friendly packaging in the market.

How to carry out a market study

1. Establish the goal for your research.

Businesses may carry out market research for a variety of reasons. They may be used to minimize problems, generate opportunities, or evaluate company risks (such as threats).

You may reduce future dangers by studying prior issues. Additionally, examine previous achievements to determine what has to be done moving forward.

Determine if the analysis is for internal or external goals before doing any market research. Internal goals might include enhancing business operations or financial flow. One of your external goals is to persuade lenders to provide you a company loan.

A crucial component of any small business strategy is your analysis. It demonstrates to lenders that you are an expert in your field and that there is room for expansion in your company.

The objective of your analysis determines the kind of research you perform. Let's take an example where you do our research for internal use. You probably won't need to gather as much data as you would for an external purpose since it's for internal usage.

Before starting your research, make it crucial to ascertain if it will be an internal, external, or combined study.

2. Examine your company's future prospects.

Describe the present situation in your industry in your analysis. Provide the industry's future direction utilizing data on size, trends, and anticipated growth. Make sure you have relevant evidence to support your assertions.

This segment will demonstrate to lenders or investors that you have done your research on the industry that your firm is in. It will also demonstrate to them if investing in your industry is worthwhile.

3. Identify your target market.

In actuality, not everyone will become a client of yours. However, that's OK! The first step in doing a market analysis is identifying your prospective clientele. We refer to this stage of the procedure as the target market analysis.

You must have a thorough understanding of your clients' backgrounds and identities. Your investigation needs to provide a precise image of your possible clientele. Consider items like as:

- Years old.
- earnings.
- gender.
- Where.
- Work profession.
- degree of education.
- status of marriage or family.

Once you've narrowed down your target market, learn about their demographics, demands, and hobbies.

On the basis of your study, think about developing client personas as well. Numerous companies have various client personas. Create many personas to reflect your usual clients after you've compiled the attributes of various customers.

Identifying your target market can enable you to sell more effectively and better serve potential clients.

Your target market may shift or alter as your company expands. Make sure your target market is still a good match for your company by periodically reviewing it.

What is the role of QuestionPro in market research?

A software platform called QuestionPro helps businesses do several kinds of market research. To produce, disseminate, and evaluate surveys and other research methodologies, it provides market research tools. There are many ways in which QuestionPro may help firms with their market research:

QuestionPro is a comprehensive survey builder that enables businesses to create their own questionnaires, include questions, and choose from a range of question formats, including multiple choice, open-ended, and rating scales.

Data collection: With QuestionPro, businesses may gather information via email, pop-up windows on websites, mobile devices, and online surveys. Additionally, it offers a range of techniques for gathering data, including targeted, random, and panel sampling.

Data analysis: QuestionPro provides a range of data analysis tools, including cross-tabulation, descriptive statistics, and inferential statistics, to help businesses extract insights from their data.

Real-time data reporting: QuestionPro offers real-time data reporting, enabling businesses to keep tabs on the status of their studies and alter their survey designs as necessary.

Integration with other tools: To provide businesses a complete picture of their market research data, QuestionPro interfaces with a number of other technologies, such as Salesforce, Google Analytics, and Zapier.

QuestionPro provides companies with a thorough platform for market research so they can learn important information about their rivals, target market, and industry trends. It helps companies to take well-informed choices based on insights gleaned from data.

How to Present Analysis and Research on the Market

After completing your analysis and research on marketing, you'll probably be asked to present your results. If you're comfortable with market research methodologies but find public speaking intimidating, here are a few easy tactics to help you become more comfortable with it:

1. Highlight Crucial Takeaways

Emphasize the most significant discoveries to prevent your audience from becoming overloaded with information. Stay with the material that addresses their top goals; they don't need or want to hear every detail that your investigation uncovered. If someone asks for more background or specific information, be prepared to provide it; but, keep the main points of your presentation front and center.

2. Employ data visualization

Using software, data visualization entails presenting large volumes of information graphically as dashboards, pie charts, graphs, and so on. Your results may be communicated to a variety of groups in realistic and interesting ways by using visual aids, such as clients, stakeholders, and corporate leadership.

3. Recount a Story

To further engage your audience and leave them with lasting impressions of your research, structure your presentation as a narrative, or tell a tale. Inspire inquiries from your audience. This keeps them engaged, transforms your presentation into a cooperative conversation, and enhances your performance as you provide them clear solutions that meet their demands.

4. Expand Your Knowledge with Marketing Research and Analysis

A successful job in marketing requires having up-to-date knowledge since the field is always evolving. Your proficiency in marketing strategy, marketing technology, social media marketing, email marketing, search engine optimization, and marketing analytics will be enhanced by the extensive curriculum of SCU's online Master of Science in Marketing program.

With a faculty composed of industry experts and designed to fit the schedules of working people, the program offers networking opportunities to help you learn about industry trends and best practices.

Motives behind market research analysis

The following justifies the analysis of market research:

1. Strategic planning is aided by the analysis of your marketing research, which may provide insights into the financial health of your business and areas for improvement, including new projects or market expansion. You may assess each possible plan's strength and ascertain its strategic advantages.

2. Determines trends: To keep up with the shifting wants of your clientele, an analysis of your market research will assist you in spotting trends in the goods offered by your rivals as well as in your own sales. Depending on when you do your study, you may be able to spot pertinent trends ahead of your rivals and maintain a competitive edge.

3. Clearly states your stance: You may position your product or brand in respect to your competition by analyzing the results of your market research. Gaining a deeper comprehension of your offering in relation to other brands or items can help you decide how to effectively present yourself to prospective clients.

4. Business predictions forecasts: By examining your market research, you may get a sense of what your company's potential future holds. To forecast future growth for your firm, you may compare data regarding trends and competitors with the anticipated outcomes from your strategic goals.

Chapter 7: Marketing and Sales Techniques

Marketing and sales are crucial elements of every profitable business. While the sales strategy turns those prospects into paying customers, the marketing strategy concentrates on drawing prospective consumers to the firm. A solid sales and marketing plan may boost profits and foster consumer loyalty by raising brand awareness and revenue.

A good sales and marketing plan goes beyond placing some advertising and making cold calls to a list of potential customers. Research is necessary to identify your top sales prospects, understand what drives their purchases, and understand where your company fits into the industry in order to develop the best plan. The information gathered from your study will inform your sales and marketing plan.

Growth and profitability are foreseeable and under control with the correct strategy in place.

Talent, knowledge, consistency, and effort are necessary for effective sales and marketing. If your company lacks that, it's critical that you locate an outside resource to assist you in creating and putting your plan into action.

Why are sales and marketing tactics necessary? Identifying and defining marketing objectives is the aim of a marketing strategy. This covers marketing strategies for reaching the proper consumers with your product or service and for gaining and retaining a competitive edge in the market. By focusing on goals first, your team will be more in sync and you will be able to choose which initiatives and advertising campaigns to fund.

Developing the best possible route to convert interested prospects into paying clients is the aim of a sales strategy. A successful sales strategy is working closely with the prospects who are most likely to buy from you and assisting them in making the decision to begin paying for your goods or services. Strategies for converting one-time clients into recurring customers or referral sources may also be included in a sales plan.

What is included in sales and marketing strategies? Usually, the marketing strategy consists of the following:

- Vision and objectives of the company
- Proposition of value
- SWOT evaluation
- Aims for marketing
- Proactive Measures
- Essence of a brand
- Setting Up
- Customer personas
- Competitive environment

Marketing strategies that attract and retain customers

The following are typical marketing techniques used by businesses to expand their clientele, promote recurring business, and foster brand loyalty:

1. Put in Place a Referral Scheme

Referral programs are a clever method to convert contented consumers into brand evangelists. You may encourage your current clientele to tell others about your goods and services by providing prizes, discounts, or exclusive access. People trust referrals from friends and family, which makes word-of-mouth marketing very potent. Referrals from satisfied customers carry a degree of confidence that is difficult to establish via other channels. This tactic not only attracts new clients, but it also strengthens the bonds of loyalty with current ones by making them feel appreciated and rewarded for their support.

2. Make Exclusive Deals and Rebates

Discounts and special offers affect customers psychologically. They instill a feeling of immediacy and FOMO, or the fear of missing out. Prospective buyers are more inclined to buy a product if they see that it is discounted for a brief period of time. It's a time-tested marketing tactic that plays on our desire to get a good price. These sales may also be useful for marketing certain items or getting rid of extra inventory. By offering real discounts, you may persuade doubtful customers to become purchasers.

3. Upselling and Cross-Selling

Upselling and cross-selling are tactics intended to increase the value of each client interaction. Cross-selling is recommending similar or complementary items to customers in order to improve their first purchase. Conversely, upselling pushes clients to upgrade to a more expensive item or service. These tactics may greatly raise the average transaction value by taking advantage of the customer's purchase intent. When implemented correctly, they not only improve your revenue but also provide added value for your customers.

4. Boost User Experience on Websites

A great deal of time prospective clients contact your firm by means of your site. Creating a positive user experience is crucial to converting visitors into customers. This entails making sure your website is user-friendly, loads quickly, and adapts to mobile devices. Important components include well-organized product information, simple checkout procedures, and clear navigation. When users can quickly locate what they're searching for and finish their transactions, you lower conversion barriers, which boosts revenue and boosts customer happiness.

5. Organize workshops and webinars.

Workshops and webinars with educational content provide your business a stage to show off its knowledge and authority in the field. Sharing insightful knowledge, expertise, or abilities with your audience engages them and establishes your brand as a reliable authority. These gatherings have the ability to draw in curious prospective clients, which makes them an effective strategy for generating leads. When attendees have learned about your brand, they are more likely to have a positive opinion of your goods or services.

6. Make Use of Customized Content

Customizing your marketing material to each unique customer's interests and behaviors is known as content customization. You may provide offers, product suggestions, and content that is extremely relevant by using data analysis and insights from previous encounters. Customization improves the consumer experience by giving them the impression that you are aware of their wants and requirements. Customers are more inclined to interact and buy when they see offers and content that speak to them. By taking into account personal preferences, this tactic increases consumer happiness and increases sales.

7. Increase Your Market Share

Entering new markets creates opportunities for expansion. Through market research and demographic identification that complements your offers, you may reach untapped consumer populations. This tactic entails figuring out these new groups' particular wants and preferences and then adjusting your marketing and product offers to suit them. By branching out into other areas, you may increase the diversity of your clientele, lower the dangers that come with being too dependent on one area, and seize significant expansion prospects.

8. Put in place a system for customer relationship management (CRM): One effective method for managing and cultivating your client interactions is a CRM system. You may monitor interactions, consolidate consumer data, and get insights into past purchases and preferences. You may use this data to develop customer-specific marketing strategies that are highly focused. It becomes simpler to communicate individually and to follow up on time, which raises the possibility of repeat business and consumer loyalty. Improved client retention and higher sales might result from optimizing your marketing efforts with a well-implemented CRM system.

9. Enhance Your Sales Channel: The route a consumer takes from first awareness to completing a purchase is known as your sales funnel. This process must be routinely assessed in order to find any bottlenecks or areas that might need improvement. It is possible to identify potential customer dropoff points and impediments by analyzing data and consumer behavior at each level of the funnel. You may expedite the route to buy and raise the conversion rate by making adjustments and lowering friction. Consistent tuning guarantees that your sales funnel operates like a well-oiled machine, optimizing your potential sales.

10. Make Use of Influencer Collaborations: Influencer alliances take use of the popularity and reach of people who have a sizable following in your sector or specialty. Collaborating with influencers whose audience is similar to your target market can help you build trust and awareness for your company. Genuine recommendations and evaluations of your goods or services from influencers have a big impact on their fan base. This tactic broadens your audience and connects you with a preexisting group of people who are more inclined to interact and trust your brand, which will boost sales in the end.

Marketing Strategy's Significance

For companies and organizations, marketing strategy is crucial for a number of reasons.

- Gives the organization direction and coherence.
- Helps make judgments based on market analysis.
- maximizes the use of money and labor.
- sets itself apart from rivals.
- strengthens bonds and fidelity.
- increases trust and acknowledgment.

- produces growth in the company and revenue.
- proactively tackles obstacles in the market.
- permits adaptation to shifting market circumstances.
- uses data to make well-informed decisions.
- emphasizes maintaining a market presence.
- collects information to enhance services and products.
- promotes adaptability and innovation.
- takes global market growth into account.
- seeks to increase revenue.

Formulating a Marketing Plan

Known as the four Ps, the components of the marketing mix are used in a marketing strategy. These are:

1. Product: The product aspect is all about the product, what it has to offer, and how it can benefit the user.

2. Price: The cost and worth of the goods are the main factors in price.

3. Place: Place is concerned with the route that the product takes to reach its customers.

4. Promotion: All of the selling and advertising strategies used to advance a product are together referred to as promotion.

The goal of the marketing strategy is to understand the market, and it may be achieved by product testing, surveys, and research. Although industry-specific variations exist, marketing strategies often center on certain elements. Among the essential elements of a marketing plan are:

- Identify your target market.
- Establish branding standards.
- Establish marketing targets and goals.
- Establish a social media strategy.
- Ascertain brand awareness
- Assess and keep an eye on the plan

1. Define Your Target Audience: Finding and comprehending the characteristics, psychographics, and behaviors of the individuals most likely to be interested in your good or service can help you determine who your target audience is. This covers elements including age, gender, economic bracket, hobbies, morals, and shopping patterns. Your campaigns will be more successful if you can define your target audience and then adjust your marketing strategies to connect with and appeal to them.

2. Make a set of branding standards: These act as a guide for how the public will perceive your company. This comprises components like the logo, colors, font, tone of voice, images, and message of your company. By establishing precise branding rules, you can help your target audience recognize, trust, and remain loyal to your brand by ensuring consistency across all marketing materials and touchpoints.

3. Establish Marketing Goals and Objectives: Having precise, quantifiable marketing goals and objectives gives your marketing initiatives emphasis and direction. Objectives may include raising brand recognition, enhancing website traffic, producing leads, augmenting revenues, or enhancing consumer loyalty. Objectives are measurable, attainable goals that complement your overarching company objectives. They also allow you to monitor and assess the effectiveness of your marketing plan.

4. Create a Social Media Plan: Social media is now a crucial component of marketing plans because it provides a strong forum for customer interaction, relationship building, and product or service promotion. The platforms you'll use, the kind of content you'll share, the frequency of your posts, and your strategies for expanding your following and increasing engagement should all be included in your social media plan. To maximize your efforts over time, it should also incorporate techniques for tracking and evaluating social media performance.

5. Establish Brand Awareness: The degree to which your target market is aware of and recalls your brand is measured by brand awareness. It's critical to evaluate your brand's recognition at the moment and pinpoint areas in which you can raise it. Surveys, social media mention tracking, website traffic analysis, and media mention tracking are a few examples of how to do this. You may broaden your consumer base, draw in new clients, and solidify your company's place in the marketplace by raising brand recognition.

6. Assess and Track the Strategy: To make sure your marketing plan is working, it is crucial to do ongoing assessments and tracking. In order to do this, key performance metrics (KPIs) including website traffic, conversion rates, social media engagement, email open rates, and marketing campaign ROI must be routinely analyzed. Your marketing plan may be optimized for better outcomes by measuring and evaluating its performance. This will allow you to determine what is working well, what needs to be improved, and make data-driven changes.

Formulating a Sales Plan

Typically, a corporation decides on its marketing strategy before implementing a sales plan. The business methods for raising revenue are included in the sales plan. This covers a range of goals focused on expanding the client base and increasing revenue.

While developing a sales strategy involves many different elements, most plans share several fundamental ideas. A sales strategy's essential elements that may contribute to its success include the following:

- Sales objectives
- Budget for sales
- Segmenting customers
- Customer archetype
- The approach to market
- Sales communication
- ways for increasing revenue.

1. Sales Objectives: For a sales team, sales objectives are similar to locations on a map. These are certain goals that the team wants to accomplish in a given amount of time, such a month, quarter, or year. Targets for revenue, units sold, market share, and client acquisition are a few examples of these objectives. Establishing specific sales targets keeps everyone on the team engaged and helps them all grasp what they're aiming for.

2. Sales Budget: Think of a budget as a financial plan that outlines the amount of money you will allocate to your sales endeavors. This covers all costs associated with making sales, such as advertising, recruiting salespeople, training courses, travel expenditures, and other resources. Making the most of your sales efforts and managing your finances effectively are guaranteed when you follow a budget.

3. Customer segmentation: This is the process of grouping your consumers according to common characteristics such as age, region, interests, or purchasing patterns. You may better address the requirements and preferences of these various groups by customizing your sales strategy with an awareness of them. You would need distinct techniques for each demographic since, for instance, what works for young people may not work for elderly clients.

4. Buyer Persona: developing a buyer persona is similar to developing a fictional character that stands in for your ideal client. You provide this character with a name, an age, a profession, interests, and other information that aids in your understanding of their identity and goals. You may develop sales messages and techniques that connect with your clients on a personal level by developing buyer personas, which will help you better understand them.

5. Go-to-Market Strategy: Pretend that you are introducing a brand-new product to the market. The go-to-market strategy serves as your tactical blueprint for introducing and persuading your target audience to purchase the product. Pricing, distribution routes, marketing initiatives, sales techniques, and customer service plans are a few examples of what it covers. Reaching the appropriate people with the right message at the right time is ensured by a solid go-to-market plan.

6. Sales Communication: Sales message is the language you use to convince potential clients to purchase your product or service. It's similar to creating the ideal sales pitch, which emphasizes the advantages of your product or service, answers any worries or objections the client may have, and finally persuades them to buy. Effective sales message is targeted to your target audience's requirements and interests, and it is captivating and easy to understand.

7. Revenue Growth Strategies: Investing in revenue growth strategies is like sowing seeds in a garden and seeing them sprout into large, robust plants. These are the plans and strategies you use to eventually boost sales and earn more money. This might include reaching out to new customers, creating brand-new goods or services, increasing client retention, or figuring out more effective methods to promote and distribute your offers. You can make sure that your business is sustainable and successful in the long run by always searching for methods to increase income.

Chapter 8: What is social media marketing and how should your strategy be developed?

Social media marketing, or SMM, is the practice of leveraging different social media platforms, such as Facebook, Instagram, TikTok, Twitter, and others, for marketing purposes. These applications may be used to make online purchases and sales of products. For example, if your business is launching a new product, you may advertise it on any of these apps to reach a large audience. We refer to this as social media marketing. SMM is the process of interacting with consumers via direct messages and comments. Developing high-quality material to showcase the reputation of your company is also included in social media marketing.

Numerous social media analytics tools are necessary while working with social media applications. To stay current online, you also need to have strong social media skill management.

Advantages of Social Media Marketing

Inferable from its broad use and flexibility, social media marketing is a successful media for corporate advancement. Rather than other regular showcasing methodologies like radio ads, print notices and announcements, it is additionally entirely quantifiable. The following are the most eminent benefits of social media marketing.

1. Incorporate a Human Touch into Your Business: You may communicate with both existing and potential clients via social media platforms. You may "humanize your brand" and establish a stronger connection with your audience if you employ them effectively.

2. Increase Traffic: You may increase relevant traffic to your website by including links to it in all of your social media postings. This sort of traffic has the ability to change guests into purchasers and further develop your site design improvement. Search engine optimization is another important strategy for increasing traffic (SEO).

3. produce Leads: You may use social media to produce leads and conversions by using tools like Facebook and Instagram stores, direct messaging, appointment scheduling, and call-to-action buttons. Increasing leads and conversions is a certain method to boost sales.

4. Raise Brand Awareness: Social media marketing will allow you to showcase your brand whether you're a tiny or new company. It may help you clarify how you differ from (and ideally outperform) your rivals.

5. Develop connections: If you want to keep your clients around for the long run, you need to develop connections with them. Online entertainment is a compelling instrument for creating connections since it simplifies it to speak with your supporters.

The most effective method to foster marketing strategy for social media.

You might be requesting how to foster a strong web social media marketing plan. You'll undoubtedly position your business and brand for social media success if you adhere to these guidelines and make use of all the tools at your disposal.

1. Lay out targets and objectives for your organization.

Focus on your objectives for your web based social advertising efforts above anything else. Maybe increasing brand recognition is your top objective. Or maybe you want to increase your online lead generation. Set measurements for every channel you want to utilize once you've determined your objectives. You may look at measures like reach, impressions, audience growth rate, and video completion rate.

2. Recognize your target

You must ascertain your target audience's identity and points of resonance before you can create content that appeals to and motivates them. To learn more about their preferences, you may do focus groups, interviews, and surveys. Moreover it's smart to participate in some friendly turning in, wherever you look at examples and conversations connected with your image and those of your rivals.

3. Research your rivals

Ultimately, you want people in your target market to select you over your rivals. Researching competitors is crucial because of this. It may provide you with ideas for your own social strategy as well as information into what your rivals are doing on social media. It could also give you the confidence to think creatively and produce unique material that makes your business stand out. Pay attention to the information that sparks the most discussion and involvement when you research your rivals. Remember to seek out influencers within your business to get some motivation.

4. Decide which platforms to use.

Social media networks are not made equally. The best platforms for you will rely on a number of variables, such as your objectives, industry, and target audience. LinkedIn is very useful if you're a business-to-business (B2B) company looking to connect with other firms. Yet, TikTok is a good option if your clothes store sells items targeted for adolescent females. Recall that you are free to choose more than one social media network, provided that you consistently provide original, relevant information on each.

5. Create original material

It's time to put out a content plan once you've done your homework and selected the social media channels you want to use. Guarantee that each piece of content you produce mirrors the character or brand voice you need to contact your target group. Create a content schedule as well, outlining the pieces you will publish on different channels. To save time and bother, you may also wish to arrange your material ahead of time.

6. Continually report and make adjustments

There are changes you may make to your social media marketing plan. As you utilize analytics to determine what is and is not working, it will probably alter. After you've put your first social plan into action, come back often. Ensure that your engagement and content are assisting you in achieving your company objectives. If not, modify your first plan of action.

Top Social Media Marketing Techniques

There are a few recommended procedures you should adhere to in order to make sure your social media marketing plan is successful. The top companies utilize these tried-and-true best practices, and they can help your business or startup succeed on social media.

1. Vary the Content You Provide

Regular material is not any less vital than diverse content. Provide your audience a range of postings that promote your goods and services and establish you as an authority in your field if you want to keep them interested. Think about combining announcements, industry news, queries, surveys, competitions, and brief advice with how-tos.

Additionally, ensure that your material is available in a range of media, including pictures, videos, live streaming, and online shops.

2. Maintain Uniformity

Every social media platform has its own voice and atmosphere. But wherever you publish, your identity and brand need to be consistent. Posts on Facebook, Instagram, Twitter, and any other channels you use should communicate your brand's lively and modern vibe, for example.

3. Have Talks

Never undervalue the significance of having a conversation with your audience. Observe closely who interacts with your material and reciprocates with likes, comments, and shares. putting up polls, live streaming, and live questions in an effort to start discussions. Giveaways and competitions are other options.

4. Utilize Tools for Content Creation

You must share text together with eye-catching images like infographics, movies, and photographs if you want to engage your audience on social media and win them over as devoted followers. Don't worry if you don't have the luxury of an internal graphic design team to produce them. Many content creation platforms, like Canva and Freepik, provide templates that make it simple and inexpensive to produce graphics.

5. Make Use of Hashtags

In social media postings, a hashtag is a term or phrase that comes before the hash symbol to assist users in finding subjects that pique their interest. You may raise brand awareness by including hashtags into your postings. Assume you are a seller of accounting services. You may incorporate hashtags like #CPA, #tax season, and #accounting in your postings.

6. Recycle and Repurpose Content

There's no need to start from scratch if you already have some brand-related material. Content that you already have can and should be reused. Consider highlighting a client on Facebook or Instagram who has left a review. Sharing articles from the blog or press release part of your website is an additional concept.

7. Measure Success With Analytics

If you don't use analytics and monitor data, you won't be able to assess the effectiveness of your social media plan. You may monitor all platform data in one location by investing in a social media analytics package, however each social media network has its own analytics tools. You'll be able to monitor follower growth over time, clicks, comments, reach, engagement rate, impressions, shares, saves, video views, and more.

8. Examine Paid Social Media

It is worthwhile to invest some money in sponsored social media advertising if your marketing budget permits it. You'll be able to target people with your adverts who could be particularly interested in the goods and services you provide. Ads on Facebook, LinkedIn, Instagram, and Pinterest are good places to start.

9. Exercise patience

Social media marketing won't provide results right away. You will, however, undoubtedly succeed if you are persistent and patient. Just be sure to provide engaging material, engage with your followers often, and target the appropriate demographic.

Chapter 9: KPIs, or Key Performance Indicators, to Help Grow Your Business

Key Performance Indicators (KPIs), which provide quantifiable goals for tracking and assessing performance, are essential for promoting corporate development. These indicators serve as benchmarks, enabling businesses to establish clear objectives and monitor their progress toward them.

Organizations may pinpoint areas for development and make data-driven choices to maximize their plans by establishing defined KPIs.

By offering a framework for gauging achievement, KPIs also help firms remain growth-oriented. They operate as standards by which performance can be measured, assisting businesses in assessing their current situation and determining the necessary course of action to meet their goals.

Businesses may guarantee that everyone is working toward the same goals by aligning their efforts towards similar objectives via the use of well-defined KPIs.

When choosing the appropriate key performance indicators, what matters?

You must first identify your audience in order to choose the appropriate KPIs for your business. In most circumstances, the human resources department will not find value in link hits, but they may be a helpful measure for social media or website managers.

Second, make sure your objectives are clear. In addition, your objectives ought to be quantifiable, achievable, and reasonable (using other KPIs). For your statistics to really demonstrate trends, measure important performance indicators across appropriate time periods.

Finally, refine and advance your KPIs. Modify or eliminate a key performance indicator if it doesn't appear to be helpful. You don't want to provide your staff with excessive amounts of useless information. Visualizations are often a more effective means of conveying crucial information and may provide profound insight.

Key phases in the process of determining key performance indicators:

While every circumstance is different, there are a few things you can anticipate when it comes to goal-setting, KPI establishment, and evaluation. Recall that gathering and converting KPI data is a continuous endeavor.

Step one

Choose some key performance metrics that are relevant to your business. This might also apply to a division or department of your business. Department heads should be consulted since they will be monitoring data and making adjustments in the future.

Step Two

Provide a user-friendly method for measuring and recording the data. The outcomes of KPIs may be shown on dashboards, scorecards, or graphs.

Step Three

Analyze the information derived from the KPIs. Assess the level of satisfaction (or lack thereof) of your business demands. Recall that the goal of KPIs is to discover how to make your business better. While analyzing the data from your key performance indicators, take your time and be careful.

Step Four

Modify tactics and procedures to boost output. Considering your key performance indicator data, consider the following:

- Adjustments that must be done
- Where do good achievements appear?
- Wherever your possible weaknesses may be. Next, take action. Make adjustments and note any changes you see.

Step Five

The next stage is to determine if your KPI targets still correspond with the overarching objectives of your department or organization. If not, think about modifying them to meet your evolving requirements.

Keep in mind that the KPI process may be continuous.

In order to get the most of this data, make sure that you keep refining your key performance indicator procedure. This might accelerate the growth of your company.

ESSENTIAL KPIs TO WATCH FOR BUSINESS GROWTH

Businesses must monitor a variety of KPIs in order to experience continuous growth and development. A portion of the more significant ones are listed below:

1. NET PROFIT MARGIN

The amount of money left over after all direct expenses of manufacturing products or services are subtracted is known as the gross profit margin. It is an essential measure of financial well-being. A larger margin indicates a larger safety net for supplementary costs and investments, guaranteeing the business continued profitability. A declining or low margin might be an indication of price or production-related inefficiencies or problems.

2. Expenses for marketing

It is essential to monitor the funds allotted for marketing initiatives, such as digital and advertising campaigns. Not only is quantity important, but so is quality of expenditure. Effective marketing spending raises sales and builds brand recognition, while wasteful or poorly targeted investment may deplete funds with nothing to show for it.

3. SUGGESTIONS

The company's staffing and financial capability for potential initiatives is shown by the Proposals KPI. By keeping an eye on proposals, businesses may modify their plans in response to the king and volume of submissions, guaranteeing that they are in line with their goals and company capabilities.

4. BUSINESS GROWTH

This key performance indicator (KPI) compares the revenue of the current year to that of the previous year in order to assess the company's growth. A business that grows steadily is doing well; on the other hand, a business that is stagnating or declining may be having issues with sales, operations, or market strategy.

5. RUNNING EXPENSES

Running costs include things like labor, utilities, and rent. Profitability is ensured by keeping these expenses as low as possible. A company that has lower operational expenses than its rivals is more likely to see financial growth, which will provide it more flexibility and resilience to changes in the market.

6. MARKETING

The quantity of goods or services sold over time is represented as sales, also known as revenue. It serves as a clear gauge of both company success and market demand. Businesses may modify their strategy by concentrating on high-performing items or services and reconsidering those that are underperforming by tracking sales.

7. NET PROFIT

Net Income is the net profits of a business after all costs are subtracted. It serves as a clear gauge of profitability, demonstrating the firm's sound financial standing and capacity to turn a profit above its out-of-pocket spending.

8. GROWTH IN REVENUE

Revenue Growth assesses how much a business revenues have increased over a certain time frame. While decline or stagnation signals possible difficulties or market saturation, consistent positive growth shows corporate health, market demand, and successful initiatives.

9. RATE OF CUSTOMER RETENTION

This KPI evaluates the proportion of clients that a company keeps throughout a certain time frame. While a low rate raises the possibility of problems with the overall value, customer service, or quality of the product, a high retention rate signifies consumer loyalty and happiness.

10. WORKER SATISFACTION

Employee satisfaction measures the level of happiness and morale among employees. A contented worker is often more dependable, productive, and supportive of the organization's objectives. Through consistent employee feedback and polling, companies may improve overall performance, lower attrition, and create a happy work environment.

11. Expense of acquiring a customer

Customer acquisition costs, which include marketing, sales, and other related expenses, are measured by the Customer Acquisition Cost (CAC). Effective marketing and sales activities are indicated by a reduced CAC. In order to maintain profitability and long-term development, it is crucial to strike a balance between CAC and client lifetime value.

How often should KPIs be updated and reviewed?

Key Performance Indicators (KPIs) are metrics that measure how often an organization reviews and updates its operations. These metrics include the kind of business, how stable it is, and how quickly changes occur within the business. KPIs should generally be evaluated on a regular basis to make sure they are still applicable and in accordance with your company's objectives. This may entail a monthly assessment for some firms, while quarterly or even yearly evaluations could be enough for others. Achieving a balance between adapting to changing circumstances and preventing needless disturbance from too frequent changes is crucial. Furthermore, KPIs should be updated anytime there are notable changes to the business operational objectives, the state of the market, or its business strategy. Your KPIs will continue to provide insightful information about the success of your company over time if you keep up a regular review and update schedule.

KPIs tools to grow your business

1. Google Monitoring

Google Analytics is a potent web analytics tool that offers a thorough rundown of the functionality of your website. It provides thorough insights into user activity, website traffic, and conversion rates. Through the examination of metrics like page views, bounce rates, and goal completions, companies can extract valuable insights into their target audience and their website usage patterns. Conversion rates can be raised, website usability can be enhanced, and marketing efforts can be optimized with the use of this information. Google Analytics' tools, such as audience segmentation and funnel analysis, enable organizations to spot growth possibilities and make informed choices to improve their online presence.

2. HubSpot:

HubSpot is a comprehensive platform for sales, marketing, and customer support that enables companies to draw in, interact with, and satisfy consumers. For monitoring key performance indicators (KPIs) at different points in the customer journey, it provides a number of tools. HubSpot offers insights on lead generation, conversion rates, and campaign efficacy to marketing teams. To improve their sales process, sales teams can monitor metrics like pipeline velocity, deal closure rates, and customer acquisition costs. Furthermore, companies can track customer satisfaction ratings, response times, and resolution rates using HubSpot's customer service solutions, which improves client relations and propels company expansion.

3. Tableau

Tableau is a top analytics and data visualization platform that helps companies realize the full value of their data. Users may use Tableau to generate interactive dashboards and visualizations that allow them to analyze trends, spot patterns, and get new insights from their data. Tableau enables organizations to get a comprehensive understanding of their operations and performance indicators by establishing connections with various data sources, such as databases, spreadsheets, and cloud services.

Tableau gives you the ability to manage marketing campaigns, analyze sales data, and keep an eye on operational effectiveness. These tools help you make wise choices and propel your company forward.

4. Salesforce

Salesforce is a cloud-based platform for customer relationship management (CRM) that assists businesses in managing their marketing, sales, and customer support initiatives. It provides a number of tools for monitoring sales success, client acquisition, and customer satisfaction key performance indicators (KPIs). Sales teams may use Salesforce to monitor KPIs like win rates, pipeline velocity, and conversion rates in order to find areas for expansion and streamline their workflow. Businesses may also evaluate campaign performance, lead generation, and return on investment (ROI) using Salesforce's marketing automation capabilities, and customer satisfaction ratings, response times, and resolution rates can be tracked with its customer service tools.

5. Klipfolio

A cloud-based dashboard and reporting tool called Klipfolio enables companies to monitor key performance indicators (KPIs) in real-time. Users may use Klipfolio to construct customized dashboards that show data from a variety of sources, such as databases, online services, and spreadsheets. Through the tracking of key performance indicators (KPIs) including revenue, sales, and website traffic, companies may get important insights into their operations and make well-informed choices to propel development. Advanced analytics and reporting are made possible by Klipfolio's robust data manipulation capabilities and drag-and-drop interface, which also facilitates dashboard creation and customization.

6. SEMrush

SEMrush is a full-featured digital marketing toolbox that offers insights into content optimization, competitive research, and organic and sponsored search results. Businesses may monitor key performance indicators (KPIs) using SEMrush, including backlink profiles, organic traffic, and keyword rankings, to increase their search engine exposure and attract more targeted visitors to their website. Businesses may maximize the effectiveness of their content and advertising tactics to draw in and hold onto consumers by examining competition data and finding high-potential keywords. Actionable insights for enhancing SEO, PPC, and content marketing activities are provided by SEMrush's comprehensive analytics and reporting capabilities, which eventually boost website traffic, engagement, and conversions.

7. QuickBooks

QuickBooks is a well-known accounting program that assists businesses with tracking spending, creating financial reports, and managing their money. Businesses may monitor key performance indicators (KPIs) like sales, profit margins, and cash flow using QuickBooks to have a better understanding of their performance and financial health. QuickBooks gives companies real-time access to financial data and automates repetitive accounting chores, empowering them to make wise choices and spur development. In order to expedite business development and simplify financial administration, QuickBooks offers the necessary tools and insights for invoice management, bank transaction reconciliation, and financial statement generation.

8. Trello

Trello is a well-liked project management application that facilitates task organization, project collaboration, and progress monitoring for teams. Businesses may use Trello to visualize tasks, deadlines, and project milestones by creating customisable boards, lists, and cards. Key performance indicators (KPIs) pertaining to resource allocation, team productivity, and project completion may be monitored by organizations to detect bottlenecks, streamline processes, and guarantee timely and cost-effective project delivery. Trello's user-friendly design and adaptable features facilitate efficient communication, help teams remain organized, and increase project success.

9. Zendesk

A cloud-based platform for customer assistance called Zendesk assists businesses in managing customer support interactions via email, chat, phone, and social media. Businesses may monitor key performance indicators (KPIs) using Zendesk to gauge how well their support operations are working, including response times, resolution rates, and customer satisfaction ratings. Zendesk gives agents self-service, automation, and ticket management capabilities so they can provide great customer experiences and create enduring bonds with their clients. The reporting and analytics tools offered by Zendesk provide useful information for enhancing customer service procedures, seeing patterns, and promoting ongoing development.

10. Moz

Moz is a renowned supplier of search engine optimization (SEO) software and solutions that help businesses enhance their online presence and attract organic traffic to their website. With Moz, organizations can watch key performance indicators (KPIs) like organic search ranks, keyword performance, and backlink profiles to measure their SEO performance and uncover chances for improvement. By doing keyword research, monitoring competition activity, and evaluating website analytics, companies may design tailored SEO strategies to increase their search engine ranks and generate more quality prospects. Moz's array of tools and resources give practical insights for boosting website content, technical SEO, and link building activities, eventually leading to higher website traffic, engagement, and conversions.

These technologies give organizations the knowledge and capabilities required to monitor key performance indicators (KPIs), identify areas for development, and promote ongoing growth and success. Whether it's refining marketing efforts, boosting sales performance, or enhancing customer experiences, employing these KPI tools may help your business accomplish their objectives and remain ahead of the competition.

Conclusion

Business development and expansion are a dynamic, multidimensional undertaking that presents both possibilities and problems. Through the adoption of strategic planning, the cultivation of an innovative culture, and the prioritization of customer happiness, businesses may establish a strong basis for long-term growth and success. Long-term success requires a constant state of adaptation to the ever-changing market environment, astute use of the resources at hand, and acceptance of adversities as priceless chances for development.

www.ingramcontent.com/pod-product-compliance
Lightning Source LLC
Chambersburg PA
CBHW052205220526
45471CB00004B/1822